ARIANA GRANDE

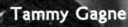

Tammy Gagne

Mitchell Lane

PUBLISHERS
P.O. Box 196
Hockessin, Delaware 19707
Visit us on the web: www.mitchelllane.com

Copyright © 2016 by Mitchell Lane Publishers, Inc. All rights reserved. No part of this book may be reproduced without written permission from the publisher. Printed and bound in the United States of America.

Printing   1   2   3   4   5   6   7   8   9

A Robbie Reader Biography

Abigail Breslin
Adam Levine
Adrian Peterson
Albert Einstein
Albert Pujols
Aly and AJ
Andrew Luck
AnnaSophia Robb
Ariana Grande
Ashley Tisdale
Brenda Song
Brittany Murphy
Bruno Mars
Buster Posey
Charles Schulz
Chris Johnson
Cliff Lee
Dale Earnhardt Jr.
Darius Rucker
David Archuleta

Demi Lovato
Derek Rose
Donovan McNabb
Drake Bell & Josh Peck
Dr. Seuss
Dwayne "The Rock" Johnson
Dwyane Wade
Dylan & Cole Sprouse
Emily Osment
Hilary Duff
Jamie Lynn Spears
Jennette McCurdy
Jesse McCartney
Jimmie Johnson
Joe Flacco
Jonas Brothers
Keke Palmer
Larry Fitzgerald
LeBron James

Mia Hamm
Miguel Cabrera
Miley Cyrus
Miranda Cosgrove
Philo Farnsworth
Raven-Symoné
Rixton
Robert Griffin III
Roy Halladay
Shaquille O'Neal
Story of Harley-Davidson
Sue Bird
Syd Hoff
Tiki Barber
Tim Howard
Tim Lincecum
Tom Brady
Tony Hawk
Troy Polamalu
Victor Cruz
Victoria Justice

Library of Congress Cataloging-in-Publication Data
Gagne, Tammy.
  Ariana Grande / by Tammy Gagne.
    pages cm. — (A Robbie reader)
  Includes bibliographical references and index.
  ISBN 978-1-68020-094-2 (library bound)
  1. Grande, Ariana—Juvenile literature. 2. Singers—United States—Biography—Juvenile literature. I. Title.
  ML3930.G724G34 2015
  782.42164092—dc23
  [B]
                                                                    2015003181

eBook ISBN: 978-1-68020-095-9

ABOUT THE AUTHOR: Tammy Gagne has written dozens of books for children, including Jennifer Lopez and Ke$ha for Mitchell Lane Publishers. She resides in northern New England with her husband and son. One of her favorite pastimes is visiting schools to speak to kids about the writing process.

PUBLISHER'S NOTE: The following story has been thoroughly researched and to the best of our knowledge represents a true story. While every possible effort has been made to ensure accuracy, the publisher will not assume liability for damages caused by inaccuracies in the data, and makes no warranty on the accuracy of the information contained herein. This story has not been authorized or endorsed by Ariana Grande.

TABLE OF CONTENTS

Words in **bold** type can be found in the glossary.

Ariana Grande sang "Bang Bang" at the 48th Annual Country Music Awards with the help of Little Big Town. The blending of their musical styles put a new spin on the hit song, which was met with great reaction from the CMA audience.

A Warm Welcome

"Shhh!" Zoe shushed her parents. They were trying to decide what to cook for dinner later that evening. Zoe had no interest—at least not in the menu. All of her attention was focused on the *TODAY* show—and the live concert that was about to begin on the plaza.

Hundreds of miles away, a twenty-one-year-old singer named Ariana Grande belted out all the hits that Zoe's family had heard blasting from Zoe's bedroom all summer. Zoe sat in front of the television, singing along. She knew the words to every one of the performer's songs.

After the concert Matt Lauer interviewed Ariana Grande. The *TODAY* host was clearly amazed by the huge number of fans who had shown up to hear Ariana sing that morning. Every spot was filled, and some people had even camped out on the sidewalk the night before. Lauer's first questions for Grande: How does she manage her enormous fame? And how does she stay grounded with all the attention she gets?

"I've spent a lot of time with my family," she told him, "and I'm very grateful for my fans and everything. It's like a blessing. I think I just have to constantly remind myself how lucky I am to do what I love . . ."

A little over two months later, Ariana would be doing what she loved in front of a different kind of audience. The setting this time was the Country Music Awards. Few people would classify Ariana's song as country, of course. But there she was singing "Bang, Bang" with the country band Little Big Town. People would be talking about the unique crossover performance for days.

Ariana was among the performers at the 2014 MTV Video Music Awards. The singer also took home the Video Music Awards for Best Pop Video.

Known almost as much for her fashion style as her music, Ariana Grande performed at the 2014 Victoria's Secret Fashion Show in London.

Beginnings and Endings

Ariana Grande-Butera was born on June 26, 1993. She spent her early years with her parents, Edward Butera and Joan Grande, in Boca Raton, Florida. Her father was a successful graphic designer there. Her mother ran a family-owned communications equipment company.

When Ariana Grande was just eight years old, she **auditioned** for the title role in a local production of *Annie*. But when she got the part, her mother was worried. "I was so young, and my mom didn't want to leave me at the rehearsals alone," Ariana told London's *Telegraph* newspaper in 2014. "But you weren't allowed to have your parents there unless they were in the show.

So my mom auditioned, which was the funniest thing that's ever happened in the history of the world!"

Apparently, the budding young actress had gotten some of her talent from her mother. Joan Grande earned herself a small part in the musical. "She was Daddy Warbucks' maid," added Ariana. "She had to wear a French maid's outfit and use a

Ariana performed two songs for the Disney Parks "Frozen Christmas Celebration." She sang "Last Christmas" and "Santa Tell Me" at the Magic Kingdom Park at the Walt Disney World Resort for the television special.

broom. She was like 'I have no idea what I'm doing right now . . . but anything for my daughter!'"

Just when Ariana's entertainment career was beginning, her parents' marriage was coming to an end. They decided to divorce that same year. Like many children in that situation, Ariana had a tough time with the change.

"Being in the middle of it was so stressful," she confided to the *Telegraph*. And of course being made up of both of them—I was like, 'Hey, if they both dislike each other's **attributes** so much, what am I to like about me? I'm made from these two people and I'm caught in the middle of all this fighting. It was **traumatic**. Between the ages of eight and eleven, that was the roughest for me."

Performing proved to be comforting for the young actress. "I remember saying, 'Mommy, I never want this to end.' I loved playing a character as it was sort of just taking a vacation from myself."

Ariana Grande helps Nickelodeon celebrate its 8th Annual Worldwide Day of Play in 2011. The event, which took place at The W Hotel in Washington, DC, gave Ariana's fans a chance to meet the star in person.

Victorious

Ariana Grande was working on Broadway at the age of fourteen. She earned a National Youth Theatre Association Award for her role in the children's musical *13*. Singing came naturally to the young performer who **possessed** a deep love of music.

"My family had exquisite taste in music and there was always music playing," she shared with *The Straits Times* in 2014. "I listened to a lot of oldies as well; my grandparents were always playing music from the 1950s and 1960s, such as **doowop**. I got a very good musical education from my family at a young age."

Ariana seemed drawn to musical roles. But she wasn't sure she was old enough to pursue a singing career just yet. "It wasn't until later on that I took singing seriously. I knew it was what I wanted to do, but I think as a young girl to get involved that early . . . it was a lot of pressure."

Ariana's older half-brother, Frankie, also works in show business. He and the rest of her family had a feeling that she would end up as a recording artist. In 2014, Frankie

Ariana's big brother is among her biggest fans. He always knew that his little sister would make it big someday.

told the *New York Times*, "She's been well on this path for years. We assumed this is where she was going."

For the moment, though, Ariana decided to stick with acting. And the strategy definitely paid off. In 2010, she was cast as Cat Valentine on the Nickelodeon television series *Victorious*. Both the show and Ariana quickly became hits.

But the experience wasn't a personal high point for Ariana. In 2013, she confided to *Seventeen* magazine, "I worked with someone who told me they'd never like me. But for some reason, I just felt like I needed her approval. So I started changing myself to please her. It made me stop being social and friendly. I was so unhappy."

Ariana Grande and costar Jennette McCurdy have some fun at the 2011 Angel Awards in Hollywood.

Jennette & Ariana

Things seemed to be looking up for Ariana Grande in 2013. After being part of an **ensemble** cast on *Victorious*, she was offered a co-starring role on a new show called *Sam & Cat*. Once again, she would be playing Cat Valentine. But the show was a combined spinoff of *Victorious* and the equally popular *iCarly*. Jennette McCurdy would continue her role of Sam Puckett from that series.

Ariana was excited to be working with Jennette. "She's the most hilarious actress I've ever met and I just adore her," Ariana told *Seventeen*. "I used to watch *iCarly* and think, 'Wow, Jennette is such a standout star and so good'. Now she's one of my best friends."

Jennette was also excited about the project. "We've been friends for a long time, before we heard about the show idea," she told MTV. "So I was excited to work with such a good friend."

Unlike much of Ariana's previous work, this show would not feature her singing. As she explained to MTV, "I don't think there's a show for kids out there now that doesn't have music."

Ariana and Jennette share a birthday. Both celebrate each year on June 26. But Jennette is one year older than Ariana. In 2013, they celebrated together on the set of their Nickelodeon television show Sam & Cat.

McCurdy agreed, "This show, I think, is about being funny and making people laugh."

Sam & Cat earned high ratings early on. It even became Nickelodeon's top-rated show during its short life. But rumors quickly began spreading about conflicts between its two stars. Stories suggested that Ariana was making considerably more money than Jennette.

Ariana denied that pay was a problem. On her Twitter page she wrote, "Jennette and I agreed upfront that we would be treated equally on this show in all regards (as we should be, considering we each work just as hard as the other on this show)." Nonetheless, it seemed that whatever problems existed, they were more than the cable network could solve. Nickelodeon canceled the series after just a single season.

Ariana spends a great deal of time performing these days. Here she is singing at the Y100's Jingle Ball in 2014.

Finding Her Voice

An old saying states that when one door closes, another door opens. This was definitely the case for Ariana as *Sam & Cat* came to an end. When she wasn't on the set, she was busy recording her first album. Titled *Yours Truly*, it **debuted** at Number 1 on the Billboard 200 chart.

Surprisingly, Ariana didn't receive her first record contract as a result of her acting roles. Knowing how talented she was, a friend sent Republic Records *YouTube* videos of her singing. After listening to them, chairman and Chief Executive Officer (CEO) Monte Lipman wanted her to sign a recording contract. Ariana decided that it was finally time to pursue her longtime passion. And apparently, her timing couldn't

Many of Ariana Grande's fans camped out on the sidewalk the night before her 2014 appearance on the TODAY Show in August.

have been better. Her second album, *My Everything*, also hit Number 1–less than a year after her first.

Ariana's determination is one of her greatest strengths. "I'm a big perfectionist!" she told *Seventeen*. "I'm trying to channel super-confident women like Alicia Keys, Mariah Carey and Beyoncé, because I realized that if you want something, you really have to go for it, just like they do."

As Lipman pointed out to *Billboard* magazine, though, striving for **flawless**ness can be a bad thing. "Because she is a perfectionist, the one thing I'll say to her every now and again is, 'Ari, perfect is not always about being perfect–it's those flaws that people can relate to."

Ariana shared with *Billboard* that she does indeed overdo it sometimes. Even back when she was performing at the Little Palm

Ariana has performed with some of the most popular people in pop music—including British singer and songwriter Jessie J.

Family Theatre in Florida, she admitted, "I just wanted to do every single show. However many there were in a year, I was in every one, whether I was a chorus girl or the lead or doing the lighting."

As much as she enjoys working, Ariana knows the importance of taking time to give back. In 2012, she and her *Victorious* cast members teamed up for the St. Jude Math-A-Thon. This education-based program raises money for children with cancer. Grande also supports the Make-A-Wish Foundation, which grants wishes

Ariana enjoys donating time to deserving charities. In 2010, she attended the Make-A-Wish Foundation Day Event in Los Angeles.

Ariana isn't just one of the most popular singers in the United States. She has quickly become an international star. In 2014, she performed at the Bambi Awards in Berlin, Germany.

for children with life-threatening illnesses.

No matter how hard she works on her music or for her favorite charities, though, many people insist on labeling Ariana a **diva**. Her response to their mean-spiritedness shows that she is no longer a little girl worried about changing to please others. "It's weird to me," she told the *Telegraph*, "because I do see myself as a fairly positive, very friendly person. So it's kind of odd. I also think a lot of people don't know what the word 'diva' means. If you want to call me a diva I'll say, 'Um, well, cool.'"

CHRONOLOGY

1993   Ariana Grande-Butera is born in Boca Raton, Florida.

2001   She stars in the title role of the musical *Annie* at the Little Palm Family Theatre.

2008   Ariana lands the role of cheerleader Charlotte in the Broadway musical *13*.

2010   She is cast as Cat Valentine on the Nickelodeon television series *Victorious*.

2013   Ariana Grande and Jennette McCurdy star in the *Victorious/iCarly* spinoff *Sam & Cat*.

        Ariana Grande releases her first album, titled *Yours Truly*

        The album debuts at Number 1 on the *Billboard* 200 chart.

2014   Ariana Grande releases her second album, *My Everything*.

        Nickelodeon cancels *Sam & Cat* after its first season.

        She wins the Blimp award at the Kids' Choice Awards for Favorite TV Actress.

        Ariana Grande wins the People's Choice Award for Favorite Breakout Artist.

        She performs at the Country Music Awards with Little Big Town.

2015   Ariana performs for the first time at the *Grammy* Awards

FIND OUT MORE

Books

Klein, Emily. *Ariana Grande, Truly Yours*. New York: Scholastic, 2014.

Morreale, Marie. *Ariana Grande*. Danbury, CT: Children's Press, 2014.

Schwartz, Heather E. *Ariana Grande: From Actress to Chart-Topping Singer*. Minneapolis: Lerner Publications, 2014.

On the Internet

Official Ariana Grande website. http://www.arianagrande.com/

Works Consulted

———. "Ariana Grande Covers 'Seventeen Magazine,' Talks Drama with former Cast-Mate." *Huffington Post*, June 25, 2013. http://www.huffingtonpost.com/2013/06/25/ariana-grande-seventeen-magazine_n_3496995.html

———. "Ariana Grande: 'If you want to call me a diva I'll say: cool.'" *Telegraph*, October 17, 2014. http://www.telegraph.co.uk/culture/music/11159510/Ariana-Grande-interview-Big-Sean-diva.html

———. "Ariana Grande is Doing Things Her 'Way.'" *Seventeen*, August 2013. http://www.seventeen.com/entertainment/features/ariana-grande-fashion-pictures-quotes#slide-1

———. "'iCarly' Stars Jennette McCurdy and Nathan Kress and '*Victorious*' Star Ariana Grande Join St. Jude Math-A-Thon Team; Help Launch Exciting New Sweepstakes." PR *Newswire*, January 24, 2012.

Caulfield, Keith. "Ariana Grande Debuts at No. 1 on Billboard 200." *Billboard*, September 11, 2013. http://www.billboard.com/articles/news/5687364/ariana-grande-debuts-at-no-1-on-billboard-200

FIND OUT MORE

Caulfield, Keith. "Ariana Grande Nabs Second No. 1 Album In Less Than A Year." *Billboard*, September 3, 2014. http://www.billboard.com/articles/news/6236678/ariana-grande-no-1-album-brad-paisley-kem

Dawn, Ranee. "Ariana Grande brings her 'Everything' to mob of fans on *TODAY* plaza." *TODAY*, August 29, 2014. http://www.today.com/toyotaconcertseries/ariana-grande-brings-big-talent-crowds-today-plaza-1D80115170

Fisher, Luchina. "Ariana Grande Speaks Out on Cancellation of *Sam & Cat*" ABC News, http://abcnews.go.com/blogs/entertainment/2014/07/ariana-grande-speaks-out-on-cancellation-of-sam-cat/

Goodman, Lizzy. "Billboard Cover: Ariana Grande on Fame, Freddy Krueger and her Freaky Past." *Billboard*, August 15, 2014. http://www.billboard.com/articles/news/6221482/billboard-cover-ariana-grande-on-fame-freddy-krueger-and-her-freaky-past

Kok, Melissa. "Everything but the diva." *The Straits Times*, September 18, 2014.

Lynch, Joe. "CMA Awards 2014: Ariana Grande Performs 'Bang, Bang' with Little Big Town in 'TRON' outfits." *Billboard*, November 5, 2014. http://www.billboard.com/articles/6304622/cma-awards-2014-ariana-grande-little-big-town-bang-bang

Musto, Michael. "Frankie Grande, Ariana Grande's Half Brother, Stars in 'Rock of Ages.'" *New York Times*, November 12, 2014. http://www.nytimes.com/2014/11/13/style/frankie-grande-ariana-grandes-half-brother-stars-in-rock-of-ages.html?_r=0

Vena, Jocelyn. "Ariana Grande, Jennette McCurdy Won't Pull A 'Hannah Montana' On '*Sam & Cat*.'" MTV, June 6, 2013. http://www.mtv.com/news/1708607/ariana-grande-jennette-mccurdy-sam-and-cat/

GLOSSARY

attributes (a-truh-byoots)–a quality belonging to a particular person or thing.

audition (aw-DISH-uhn)–a short performance to test the talents of a musician, singer, dancer, or actor.

debut (dey-BYOO)–a first public appearance.

diva (DEE-vuh)–prima donna. A principal female singer in an opera. A vain, temperamental person.

doowop (DOO-wop)–a style of pop music marked by the use of close harmony vocals using nonsense phrases, originating in the United States in the 1950s.

ensemble (ahn-SAHM-buhl)–a group of people or things making up a complete unit.

flawless (FLAW-les)–perfection.

possess (po-ZES)–to own.

traumatic (TRA-ma-tik)–an event that causes psychological shock. A distressing experience.

INDEX